# Dixmont

Rick Campbell

*[handwritten inscription:]* Therese —

This has been a night
to surpass all others —
passion, desire,
poetry, beer,
what else is there?
why can't it last?

*RC*

**Autumn House Press**

PITTSBURGH

*Autumn House Press Staff*
Executive Editor and Founder: Michael Simms
Executive Director: Richard St. John
Community Outreach Director: Michael Wurster
Co-Director: Eva-Maria Simms
Fiction Editor: Sharon Dilworth
Special Projects Coordinator: Joshua Storey
Associate Editors: Anna Catone, Laurie Mansell Reich
Assistant Editor: Courtney Lang
Editorial Consultant: Ziggy Edwards
Media Consultant: Jan Beatty
Tech Crew Chief: Michael Milberger
Intern: Rebecca Clever
Volunteer: Jamie Phillips


ISBN: 978-1-932870-17-6
Library of Congress Control Number: 2007902327

For Marcia, Della Rose, all the dogs,
cats, creeks, gardens, songs—
All that we call this land

# The Autumn House Poetry Series

**Michael Simms,**
**Executive Editor**

*Snow White Horses, Selected Poems
1973–88* by Ed Ochester

*The Leaving, New and Selected Poems*
by Sue Ellen Thompson

*Dirt* by Jo McDougall

*Fire in the Orchard* by Gary Margolis

*Just Once, New and Previous Poems*
by Samuel Hazo

*The White Calf Kicks* by Deborah Slicer
● 2003, selected by Naomi Shihab
Nye

*The Divine Salt* by Peter Blair

*The Dark Takes Aim* by Julie Suk

*Satisfied with Havoc* by Jo McDougall

*Half Lives* by Richard Jackson

*Not God After All* by Gerald Stern
(with drawings by Sheba Sharrow)

*Dear Good Naked Morning* by Ruth L.
Schwartz ● 2004, selected by Alicia
Ostriker

*A Flight to Elsewhere* by Samuel Hazo

*Collected Poems* by Patricia Dobler

*The Autumn House Anthology of
Contemporary American Poetry*, edited by
Sue Ellen Thompson

*Déjà Vu Diner* by Leonard Gontarek

*Lucky Wreck* by Ada Limon ● 2005,
selected by Jean Valentine

*The Golden Hour* by Sue Ellen Thompson

*Woman in the Painting* by Andrea
Hollander Budy

*Joyful Noise: An Anthology of American
Spiritual Poetry*, edited by Robert Strong

*No Sweeter Fat* by Nancy Pagh ● 2006,
selected by Tim Seibles

*Unreconstructed: Poems Selected and New*
by Ed Ochester

*Rabbis of the Air* by Philip Terman

*Let It Be a Dark Roux: New and Selected
Poems* by Sheryl St. Germain

*Dixmont* by Rick Campbell

*The River Is Rising* by Patricia Jabbeh
Wesley

*The Dark Opens* by Miriam Levine ● 2007,
selected by Mark Doty


● winner of the annual Autumn House
Press Poetry Prize

# Contents

# Acknowledgments

*10x3 Plus*: "(a dream I had one night in America);" "Some Notes on Other Things;" "Time Running Out on the Millennium"

*Apalachee Review*: "Meditation on the Limitation of Desire"

*The Chattahoochee Review*: "The Muse;" "Dixmont"

*The Flint Hills Review*: "The Grave;" "Intro to Lit" (as Kurtz)

*The Florida Review*: "Buffalo;" "Bad Angels;" "Fair Warning;" "Heart"

*New Madrid*: "The Body as Instrument;" "Outside Fason's Butcher Shop the Sign Proclaims Nostalgia Racers for Christ"

*Nimrod*: "For the Woman Who Left Part Way Through the Poetry Reading"

*Poets Respond to Violence*: "In a Motel in Louisiana I Watch the Pirates and the OJ Simpson Freeway Chase at the Same Time"

*Red Wheelbarrow*: "Road House;" "Kansas"

*Rockhurst Review*: "The Smokers' Room"

*roger*: "Prayer for Daily Neglects;" "Spring in the City Graveyard"

*Saranac Review*: "Trying to Save You"

*Southeast Review*: "Letters Home: Spring Storm, Santa Fe;" "Kuaa Pueblo"

*Tampa Review*: "For Marcia"

*Terminus*: "Travel. Spring. West. Elevation"

*Texas Review*: "Again, Vietnam"

*Whetstone*: "Elegy for Matthew Shepard"

# The Muse

who would have guessed, loves
to hear stories of Roberto
Clemente. In fact, she says
it makes her hot. Best baseball
player ever, handsome, passionate.
Gives his life for the poor. All
I have to do is tell Roberto
stories. Imitate Bob Prince

singing "Arriba, Arriba,"
and she's all over me.
Goddesses, as you might know,
are no slouches at love. Odysseus
spent seven years in Kalypso's
bed and even the night before he
was to sail home to Penelope
he went for a little more of that
ambrosia.

It's not easy for me to love her.
Any man knows the pressure
of performance anxiety. When
you love a goddess there's no room
for strikeouts, for guessing curve
and getting a fastball that leaves you
standing there with your bat on your shoulder.

For the muse, I invent Clemente stories
I figure even she can't have seen all the games,
not every play. I've got a library in my head,
Prince, Jim Woods, my grandfather's
embellishments.

I used to think cultural feminists were tough.
All of that talk about orgasm and power,
the way they'd whisper Shulamith
Firestone, Mary Daly, just when

you were about to steal home.
The muse doesn't say
anything. It's her silence. Her
eyes starting to wander. Suddenly
she's talking about Odysseus,
how he could swim nine days
and I tell her about the time
Clemente plays the ball off the right
field wall, 375 feet away. Turns toward home
and lets the ball fly, like O
at the Phaeacian games (I do this
to show that I can get Homer into this

game too) and it screams toward the plate
on a line, across the wine-dark grass
(she looks at me now, brows arched)
the runner from first is heading
home when the ball arrives, knee high,
on the fly. The catcher waits there like
(her look says *skip the simile*); the runner
stops and looks out to right. Smoky
walks down the line and tags him
gently. *Clemente was a god*,
I say. She says, *come here*.
One more night.

## Dixmont

The asylum my mother lived in
those long months seemed like
something from a gothic novel.
A vampire castle. Dark always.
We used to visit, maybe once
a week. I remember a waiting
room. Stiff chairs and a long
clinical hall. Slippers shuffling
down the floor. Attendant at her arm,
I remember her slow, moving
in a haze I have no name for.
We never stayed long. She left
us like a bad mother and there
was nothing she could do. As
we drove home it was unbearably
green and I was guilty of leaving
my mother behind. My father
was not sad enough. Finally
we'd reach the river and turn
for home. The heat and humidity,
buttoned down by soot and smog,
fell upon us. I don't remember this
like a photograph, but like a child
imploding. I remember this
as an attempt to remember something.
It's me there I'm trying to remember;
her, I'm trying to bring home.

## Fair Warning

These stones are from my daughter's collection,
pebbles washed in the river of days. She
asks which is my favorite and I

work against my will to say all of them are nice—
the line that means Daddy's not really paying
attention now; his mind is in another part of the house

somewhere in Clifton's poems,
or counting dollars
for the Bank of America bill.

Below my heart, where things are tight,
where I keep my father, I remember my promise
not to be him, and say this one, the one

that looks like a blue dinosaur's tooth,
and this one too, the way the dark
swirls so deep into the brown like love,

like how I look at you and know there is no excuse
for not giving the world, all your blood,
every inch of skin and bone, for your child.

Then we slide the box under her bed
and wash our hands for dinner.

## The Body as Instrument

The body can be an instrument
of measure. You stand with legs spread
firm on the earth, and stretch your arms
out to your sides, true and straight. You sight
down each arm, your body forming the 180 degree line,
and then you bring your arms together in front of your nose,
sight that line to the next horizon,
and there's the right angle you walk.
Why? Maybe you're looking for something.
Maybe plotting or plodding the boundary
of a field, or more boring, the corner
of a lot that will be like the lot like the lot
like the lot next to it. And white 3 bedroom
houses will sprout here. And palm trees
will be set here, propped up by sticks. You
walk your line; each measured time your right
foot hits the earth you add 5—a counting
rhyme in your head—5, 10, 15, 20.
You try not to vary your stride—25, 30
35, 40—because if every right foot hits true
the point you are looking for will be near
what your pacing's supposed to yield. We
took pride in measuring distance with our feet,
turning angles by hand, eyeballing plumb
without a range rod and level. Our bodies
were an act of love, a certainty more than machine.
We wanted to find our reference points, traverse
our way across field or swamp, subdivision
or highway curve, without the theodolite's
turned angles. *Let us walk* we said,
*let us lay our bodies down.*

# Road House

After the kids had gone back to town,
to rock and roll bars and bodies
like their own, the owner
would unplug the jukebox

and start his reel of favorite songs.
Popcorn was free and sometimes beer too.
And we'd listen, And we'd dance.
And he'd sit and tell us some story

we were privileged to know by heart
because all good stories are already ours.
After midnight, I'd look up at the bar,
the neon beer signs, a dead elk on the wall.

The fat man I imagined sad, long eyes
of a Basque sheepherder, would look at his wife
sleeping on the bar, head in her arms,
and then whisper to his dog—who waited for this moment—

*wanna dance.* Between bar and empty tables
he'd wrap his big arms around the mutt and sway
in the yellow light. They danced a slow circle,
no matter what the music said.

## For the Woman Who Left Part Way Through the Poetry Reading

What is it that won't wait until 3:30
on a warm winter afternoon? I wonder if you think
you've been imprisoned, if the air
and sun outside promise a freedom
so rare that a few more poems are a weight
so heavy and gray that behind
your eyes, the poems rise slowly
and inexorably as the tide. Tannin
dark water seeps into the room. You
want to scream *look out. Get out. Now.*
But you can't scream here so you shift
in your chair; your sneakers rest on the rail
of the chair in front of you, but the water
is rising fast. You're up; you're running
toward the sun, the world outside that is bright
and dry, where no words fall like forty days
of rain, and the dove in your heart returns
to roost in the branches of the blossoming dogwood.

# Imaginary Numbers

## 1.

In high school algebra I decided not to believe
in imaginary numbers. It seemed my right.
Who could force me to believe in Peter Pan,
to resurrect my lost Santa Claus, to put
my family back together, make love,
loyalty, and honesty inviolable virtues
again? I didn't care to solve for X and Y.

RBI maybe. Or the number .351, Clemente's
batting average. I liked 9, the bottom of,
2 outs, 2 on, 2 strikes. The symmetry of that
& maybe imagining me driving a ball into the gap,
10 feet from the outstretched glove of either fielder,
the ball 2-hopping the 325 sign. These imaginary
numbers I could live with. I told Mrs Whoever
Was There Then, in the geometry of the institutional
green classroom that I would not figure her imaginary
numbers.

The numbers on the clock were real enough;
I could do long division in my head and make
change for a dollar. Even the supposedly more real
polynomials, the simplified factors
that lived on both sides of an equation
were lines less real than the railroad
tracks that split black from white in our small
coastal town.

2.

Long after my denial of algebra
sent me to the Dean's office, where
abstract infraction was added to my
dismissal of socks, my advocacy of
a woman's right to wear blue jeans,
to the number of times I'd been cited
for my hair falling over my shirt collar,
I was in a field of palmetto scrub
with a survey crew. Our efforts to find
a property line, an iron pipe, a monument,
something we were looking for with chains
and machete tips, had proven futile. Our party
chief, maybe a bit too drug-addled and Vietnam-
weary to remember, said "what's that theorem,
that formula for finding things, triangulating?"

I heard again the hollow echo, the soft voice
in the green room, and I said Pythagoras,
$A^2+B^2=C^2$. We had the numbers
in our hands. $A$, we'd chained from a tintab
in the street, $B$ pulled from a good corner. We squared
them, worked the numbers, turned the angles.
We walked the line with our chain and there it was.
For a moment, maybe a whole afternoon, I believed
in algebra, in all its magic and alchemy. But the day
ended, night washed over us, and then the next day
and the next day followed.

# Ghost Counselor Explains His Craft

Ghosts are not like you and me.
Less corporeal, more nimble,
they flit while we walk,  float
while we leap. They do not
talk but implant their words
faster than memory, slower
than light.

Ghosts often forget where they are
or where they were going. They forget
their limitations, reaching out to touch
their lover, their child, even an apple
red on the plate. I help them
readjust, come down to earth
in a way, a way they can't ever come down:
free of gravity, friction, free
of all resistance but their lost desire.

Ghosts are not wood, stone, mist
or water. Ghosts are not air,
but it helps to imagine them so.
The ghost who loves you, misses your touch;
the ghost who cannot leave your side,
your house, your dark street—
needs you to touch her, to say
goodbye. The problem's always
in that touch. She reaches
and passes through you. You
don't reach but long to. You
try to reach and hold and hold
some more.

The ghost who loves you
needs you, but you can never meet.
This is our world; the seer and I
make a bridge; we believe
in the ghost who loves you.

But there's no proof of anything,
no evidence to send home
in a manila envelope. You
thought you were done with faith
when she died. For her,
it's only begun.

# A Poem for Della                    *5/16/01*

Sometimes, still, she wakes and says,
*Daddy I have to go to the bathroom,*
and I pick her up. She's warm.
She wraps her arms around my neck,
her legs around my waist, and I carry her.

We used to sit, she wrapped
in a baby blanket in my arms
in the garden, and I would watch
the sun rise above the trees.

She would sleep, but I think
still knew the sun's coming
by the changing light, the warmth
rising, it seemed not from the sky

but from the woods, the creek,
the wild roses. She sleeps
in her bed now. She walks alone,
but wakes still with the first light

and rises new into the day. She
does not remember that I carried her
to the bathroom last night, that
I covered her up as her head fell

to the pillow. She doesn't
think that somewhere, maybe
Eastern Europe, the Aegean,
the Azores, the sun was rising,

beginning its journey to her
to us, to us all

## For Marcia

The sky is gray and low—too
warm for fog, too solid for rain.
When the wind blows, drops of dew
shuffle down to clatter
on my tin roof and spatter
on the dry leaves. I'm in the tenuous space
of my wife's sadness, that worm
that ravels through her brain, talking,
whispering, that neither drugs nor sunlight,
the garden or our daughter's eyes
can fully quiet. Yesterday
she shattered the window
and banged her head on the wall
because I had triggered the car alarm
and couldn't shut it off.
Last night she was back, smiling,
but sad behind the smile, as we sang
"Rockin' Robin, tweet tweet"
and Della danced. I don't know
what to do. Rain means weeks
of drought have broken, means
the garden will live. Fog
means the world will come more
softly rounded today.

## In a Motel in Louisiana I Watch the Pirates and the OJ Simpson Freeway Chase at the Same Time

Stan Musial meets the Emperor of Japan
as OJ, with his gun to his head
is driven down the LA freeway,
cop cars following, choppers above,
and NBC's cameras live, showing us a white
Bronco in a solitary parade, as if the mere
image of a car on a freeway was news and
everyone is worried that OJ might shoot
himself as the cops show more restraint
than they showed Rodney King
or than OJ showed his wife,
and just then the Pirates turn a sweet
double play. The Emperor and his wife
don't cheer, maybe out of deference
to their host. Maybe they aren't fans. Stan
the Man stays in the shadows at the rear
of the luxury box so we don't know if he
curses the Cardinal batter who could
not lay off the sinker low and away.

# History

The sun in the canopy, the rain
beating the sandy soil, running
down the gullies of the driveway
is the history of yesterday.

Last week was the history of codeine,
of root canal and the longer history of its payment.

The history of swimming
with my daughter as she showed
that now she can swim in the deep end.
The history of her bobbing up, breathing,
going down, bobbing, breathing.
The history of me floating on a noodle,
because I don't tread water well,
as she bobs, so that I can reach out and grab her
if this bobbing does not work.

This week's a history of grass
growing tall after rain, which was the end
of the history of drought. The history
of weeds is a foot higher
than the history of grass, today.

The history of grass changes quickly,
like the history of Iraq, of being welcomed
with open arms, reasons
for justifying war. The history
of the lawnmower is the history of the future
but the future isn't what it used to be.

The history of the lawnmower
will challenge the history of quiet—whose

history is already challenged by the philosophy
and politics of perception.
Quiet not as the absence of sound
but the nature of sound. Birds singing,
a first glow of cicadas,
frogs distant enough to be rumble
and punctuation, squirrel flutter
in high leaves, random water drops
on a tin roof.

The history of our domestic week is small—
no assassinations, no car bombs, no
Campaign against Fallujah. No children
beaten in boot camps. No governor's
press conferences. No earthquakes,
tornadoes, hurricanes, tidal waves.
No planes crashed into tall buildings.

# Meditation on the Limitation of Desire

In this morning of cardinals
the neighbor's cattle low
and a dog—who knows its master?—
wails like a penitent awakened
not from nightmare, but just another
night's dream.

The cardinals are constant.
Warblers intermittent. Woodpecker
a surprise, each drumming new
and unexpected. Behind this,
every few minutes, a dove coos.

All of this seems now destination.
As if, like the armadillo
diligently shuffling through the brush
toward our garden, I too
have long been seeking this soil,
its grubs and worms.

Sometimes we stretch the metaphor
too thin, our artifice transparent
as the locust husks clinging
in afterlife to the loblolly's rough bark,
its darker sap. In this desire
to make ourselves one
with the world outside our skin
and blood, our frail but impassable
barriers, we miss the obvious—
that it is desire for the armadillo,
the hawk high in the soft sky,
the sun not yet fully above the trees
that makes us what we are,
not less than the song,
but someone listening, someone
wanting to sing.

# Spring in the City Graveyard

*for Rhonda*

...Who hasn't lodged in the belly
of something, who hasn't been devoured?
Frank X. Gaspar

When we walk in the graveyard
are we closer to death or farther away?
This is in anticipation of what? The next meal,
the next kiss, the next farewell? Who has not wondered
if this sky is the same one floating over
Budapest or Providence? If Duluth is closer
to God's sovereign gaze for being closer
to the Pole. When we walk among the stones
and tombs, we know that slaves are buried
elsewhere; some marked as property;
some just a swelling, a sinking, in the ground.

I'm calculating how to repair all that's lost
and broken. My friend's dead in Utah. I've
been wallowing lately—feeling I've brought
too much on myself, I sit and sigh before
cop shows and crime. But spring's coming in the dogwood's
thousand buds swelling toward blossom.
This should be enough to save me
from the small animal I've allowed
this purchase on my heart.

## Duck Fight, Lake Ella

The old man in the Swingin' Sammy
Snead hat jogs to the shore and claps
like a kindergarten teacher—*now now*—
*ducks, ducks, ducks*. The little
girl says the ducks are fighting. The old man
says the black and white is going to kill
the other and I'm thinking that I don't know
much about ducks mating, but if this is it, count me out.
The *über* duck's on top, wings beating, forcing
the *sub* duck under water. Then the under duck is free
and I don't know if we've had copulation
or just one duck bullying another. Maybe both,
I figure. I know more about dog genitalia, but
when was the last time you saw a duck on its back,
all four legs akimbo, rolling its shoulders
on the ground or something worse,
little pecker out for all the kids to see.
I walk around the lake again.
All the ducks are in a row.
Perhaps a territorial détente has been reached, or maybe
this is the ennui after sex and someday
there will be another duck on Lake Ella;
someday, in a duck's gestational time.

## Kansas

Three A.M. The 7-11 light
puddles in the parking lot
and spills greasy into neighboring
fields. Lost, we ask the clerk
where U.S. 50 left us wandering
in this town that smells like an
augury of Dodge's stockyards
and slaughterhouses. He's scared,
even in Kansas clerks know
that death walks in the wake
of two men strung out
from all night driving,
eyes bright as cheap vodka.

*Down the road, second left,*
he says. *No one uses it anymore.*
*You should be on the Interstate.*
We don't kill him. He takes
his reprieve seriously and shines
the counter like it's a saint's relic,
a good luck charm against the dark,
the headlights still coming
down the old road's lost life.

## Intro to Lit

Wife and daughter gone a week
I revert to the nature of men.
Clothes litter the floor.
Dog hairs on the couch.
I have painted a stick girl
on my t-shirt with a cherry pit.
Like all men, with too much power,
the Romans, all presidents and kings,

on the eve of impending battle
I think I can find my better angel
the day before they come home.
I'll gather cleaning supplies,
do the laundry, sweep, vacuum.
I dangle over the precipice
and it's always too late.
Testosterone tends toward

disorder and delay. Left alone
I have no morals to sustain.
Cleanliness, though still next to Godliness,
is far from me and I am far from God.
I could be closer to Greek Gods
I suppose—petty, self-interested,
amoral. Consider Apollo
outside the gates of Troy

slaughtering the Argives, or
Athena savoring Odysseus' arrows
stuck through the throats of the suitors.
I can't imagine Zeus cleaning up
after himself—consider the mess

he made of Leda, or the golden shower
dripping on Danae's floor. The

flood of lies he told Hera
that became mythology,
that untidy cosmology with Chronus,
his father, his balls cut off,
thrown into the sea. Aphrodite.
One more day till they return.
It's only this which saves me—
Duty. Obligation. Fear

of Chastisement. My God,
if I had one, would be Old Testament,
Puritan, a God whose Vengeance
and Fickleness are written larger
and more often than Mercy.
Today I will drive to Wal-Mart,
buy a mop and bucket, something
shiny, on wheels, the kind

with a wringer that ratchets
down tight on the long-stringed mop
squeezing the dirt-dark water.
I need a new tool to make me
a better man, though sometimes
trying to transcend my sloth
I wonder why there isn't another
option, not Man, not Woman,

not janitor, not maid.
Not God, not Goddess,

just someone, something
that, like an apple ripens,
like a sunflower turns to the sun,
knows the Good, doesn't need
Shame, or Fear, or Reward
to lift him to a lofty perch.

## Again, Vietnam

In the stubble of a frosted beanfield
black birds dance in the sparkle of ice.
We see only the silhouettes, nothing precise
as the tractor summer nights that steels
its light against our pines, whose drumming wheels
above our heads like carrion birds that twice
sang their bitter song in the green paddy's rice
we never think we want to hear or feel.
That was a life lost long ago, a sound
that now I hear in the silence rising
from the long cut rows of soy that draw
a flock of black-cloaked peasants bent to ground,
bobbing their quick-heeled souls across a thing
better left to dark and moon; the things I saw.

## Naming Things

*after Garcia Marquez*

Before we forget
what most things are
we can write the names
on cards and tape them
to the trees, table, shed,
pumphouse. Naming the dogs,
hawk, squirrel, will be harder.
Verbs will be hardest of all.
How to tape a card on *walk*
or *fly*, *drink* and *breathe*.
The dog might sit still
long enough to get marked
*dog*, but what of *dig, bark,
scratch*? We'll need movies,
records of our lives in motion,
but that too will need a card
marked *camera*, and another
marked *scenes*, and another
that tells us why we want to know
this about ourselves. Then, captions:
*this is the dog running*. We
will have a problem with *this* and *is*.
There could come a day when we forget
all, forget day and night. Why day
is light and night not. Why we work
in one and sleep in the other. Who
will feed the thing marked *dog*?
Who will remember what it means
to feed? The card for sky

will fall to the ground marked *earth*
and someone else will have marked it
*soil*, someone *dirt*. There will be
a pile of cards, a scattered list of what
we used to know. We will have forgotten
*know*; the card for rain will be wet,

but that we will have forgotten too.
The card for wind will have a picture
of trees bent and swaying, but the card
for trees will have been lost. Bent
and swaying will be motions we
never understood.

## Intelligent Design and the Click Beetle

The Latin sounds like something it's not.
*Elater*. One who elates. One who makes
us elated. Say instead, *click beetle*, a name
as sonorously accurate as others
are false—the ant lion, which is neither,
the horse fly, which is no horse;
the praying mantis, which offers no words
to God. But the click beetle, the vernacular
dead on—a loud click, the snap
of a mousetrap that catches nothing.
What makes it thrust its articulated body
so violently that it throws itself in the air
twenty times the leap of Michael Jordan?
Who measures these things?

But unlike Jordan or the humble
hated flea's leap, the click beetle
accomplishes little. Just
leaps to turn over; clicks, leaps
flies a foot in the air out of desperation,
in the hope that its chance landing
will plant it on its feet. What are the odds?
Heads: tails. Belly: back.

The beetle clicks, leaps, falls, assesses its heads
or tails state, then either crawls off somewhere
or  begins again. If grand design
were measured by a success ratio, wouldn't
a simple rollover mechanism be a better idea?
The universe is full of little jokes and games

of chance. I had only a minute chance of getting
throat cancer and I got it. Then I had a 90% chance
of being cured, and maybe I am. The
odds were so slim that the drunk
who hit my wife's car that afternoon
on a lonely country road
would be speeding east as she drove west
on a blue May day.

What are the odds that the next snake under
the mulch hay is a copperhead, not an oak?
Or that the prop plane overhead will make it
to the next little landing strip? Maybe
the god that designed the click beetle
is a betting man. Maybe he's the same one
who wagered Lucifer over Job's steadfastness?
If he'd bet a man's children, stock, luck and life,
then whether the click beetle lands heads or tails
hardly seems striking or cruel. Click, heads—
we walk away. Click, tails—we roll into the ditch.
Click, heads—the doctors save us. Click, tails—
> They don't.

## Outside Fason's Butcher Shop the Sign Proclaims Nostalgia Racers for Christ

When I tell my daughter about the wounds
I say Roman soldiers with long
pointed spears jabbed him
when he was on the cross. I pick
Roman soldiers because essentially
Romans could represent nostalgia,
especially to a five-year-old
in the year 2000, and soldiers
no matter who or where or when
can be believed to jab someone

with spears. It's the nature
of their mission. I skip the part
of the story with the nails
in the palms. I skip the part
about being God—Mary's son,
that's enough. Mary the Great Mother
who in our house sees and protects
and brings babies to those who wait
ten long years on earth.

Now as I pass the sign
I wonder if these are old stock cars
roaring around a dirt track—Tbird,
Charger, Cougar, Chevelle
396—out somewhere
in the paper mill pines,
and if these are old motorheads
driving old muscle cars,
remembering an old time religion
of slamming through gears
and slick wide tires.

If their Christ was better then,
if it's the Christ of the Firebird
mourning the coming of Camrys,
minivans and SUVs,
if one needs the Cobra Jet 429,
the 396, the Hemi, roaring
glasspacks and a Hurst on the floor,
fast cars giving themselves to Jesus.

Each day I see this sign
and think of racing cars
and the haunches of pigs,
the ribs of cows, thick cut bacon,
sausage, of entrails washed
out to slop, of blood dripping
to the sand.

# The Smokers' Room

Encased in glass
the terminal smokers
sit, some staring
straight ahead, others
turned to the window
that looks over the parking
lot and four tiers
of garage. No one
talks. Time
is short. Their flight,
no smoking. They've promised
children who want to see them
breathe deeply. But here
for these moments, they
are free. Everyone is locked
in the same rapt embrace.
They are rare animals
at the zoo. The next terminal
waits in the rain.

## Click Beetle II

The roach tightly encased in the spider's web
could be a piece of lead, like the weights
placed on a rim for balance.
I pick it up and it snaps like those frog clickers.
I drop it, pick it up again.
It clicks again as if a charge
runs through its body.

I rub its belly; it clicks again, head
snaps upright and falls back. I rub it again.
It clicks and falls. This is a parlor game.
an experiment. Inside the death cocoon
the roach is alive. I rub it like an incantation
and this time it leaps a full foot in the air
and falls back to window sill.

I can't get enough. I want this roach
to outlive civilization here in my gazebo.
I spin it like the needle of a board game
and remember Eberhart's line that "God
does not live to explain." My roach
slowly climbs the screen, his legs work free
and he trails the web like a wedding gown.

It's slow, reintroducing itself to a world
only moments ago thought lost.
A moth lands on the screen. Nothing
in my meager knowledge
of bug world makes the moth
a predator of the roach. So I get up close
to watch and I think the roach is a beetle.
I see that the moth is tethered by thread

too. The beetle I stroked back to life
becomes the predator. Two black dots ringed
with white on top of its head, a jointed
carapace where head meets body. I value it
more as a beetle, like the squirrel's worth more than the rat,
hawk more than vulture.
Neither the moth nor the beetle is moving

now, and my interest wanes. I could kill
the beetle and set the moth free. I could
bottle them both in my daughter's collection.
I drink more coffee, noting that I've interceded
enough for one morning, but my tender heart
can't leave the moth tied to the screen, so I cut it loose,
and it flies to my cheek,  brushes
my beard, my hand, and is gone.

## To All Those Who Prayed for Me

It seems wrong. For years,         *Hail Mary full of grace*
maybe since the second I kissed
the Bishop's ring
on the cold steps of St John's,
I have not believed in prayer
or its God. I said a few more
after that day, most coerced
by threat or promise of penance.

Even grace I subscribed first
to the flight of a ball and the intersection
of a glove deep in the gap, then the lines
of a trout hovering in an eddy
of the Encampment river.

*The Lord is with thee*

Those I see who touch my arm
and say they've asked their God,
whole congregations of Baptists
or Methodists I don't know praying
for me, a candle flickering for me,
a list I'm on of those who need God's favor

*Blessed art thou*
*amongst women*

I still don't believe, but I turn
no one, no prayer, no whispered
or chanted words, away. In
the midst of drought, the first rain

39

falls in splatters, pops the thick dust. I
don't believe prayer brought it. I don't
believe god's watching the smoke
from a votive candle with my name
on it work its way to heaven
like the mother of all emails.

*And blessed is the fruit of*
*thy womb, Jesus*

And I am, wrapped in the love
of wife and daughter.
I used to say this:

*Holy Mary, Mother of God,*
*pray for us sinners,*

but I didn't believe
in sin either. I believe
in songs: *Make me an angel*
*that flies from Montgomery,*
seems closer to prayer. I smile
and thank the faithful, thinking
it's not the first time I've crossed
or bordered on hypocrisy. I believe
in believing in something.

As the cancer goes away and my voice
returns, I tell them it must have worked,
their prayers, the woodpecker in the dead
loblolly, the red tailed hawk floating
the blue sky.

Hail Mary, Hail Della
Holy Ohio, Holy Sewannee, Oclocknee,
Aucilla, Wacissa. Mother of God.
Mother of my daughter. Mother of petroglyphs
and dolphin rising in the morning sun.

*Now and at the hour*
*of our death*
*Amen*

# Buffalo

In the yard where the buffalo fetish
fell, I walk back and forth, tracing
the steps I must have taken
behind the lawn mower. My blue
buffalo gone, only the rawhide
reminder of my adopted clan
clings to my neck.

I walk the grass and weeds, clover
and buckwheat. I step over ant hills,
look where the lawnmower's stored,
where I'd pulled the starter rope.
There is no more buffalo. Buffalo
Bill shot them from a passing train.
Buffalo soldiers fought Indians.
Buffalo grazed here when Bartram
walked the Florida savannah.
Buffalo, my wife says, lived
in South Park, in Pittsburgh, when
she was a child.

Once, years ago, I drove my Ford
through Custer State Park, grass
rolling as far as I could see, and then
the buffalo, thousands of buffalo
crossing the road. We stopped
and buffalo flowed past us
like a slow shaggy river. Great
heads low, they walked around us
as if we were a stone.
Thirty minutes of buffalo.

Now, fetish gone, I walk back
to the house. Years from now
my grand kids will find a stone
and say, *Mom, look, a blue
buffalo.* I hope Della
remembers this and ties you,
Grandpa's lost buffalo,
last of a kind, a ghost dance of love,
tightly around a neck I've
maybe never seen.

## Some Notes on Other Things

Somewhere on a weather map
where a satellite photographs
our house and the dogs sleeping
in the yard, rain rattles leaves.

A tropical storm rides the Apalachee
coast. Landfall today, somewhere between
the Aucissa and Cedar Key. Rain coming
to swell our swollen creeks, Telogia
already encroaching the highway.

The soup has settled here.
Sycamore. Absent from
most maps, too small for a dot
on a road map, we can be seen
from space, by satellite, by god
as we sit here, Friday, in the path
of a slow, wet storm.

Gray slows the morning;
even the copperhead I killed
two hours ago is old news.
The quick rise I get when I bring
the blade down on its neck,
the fear that this snake will
close the distance between him
and my calf faster than my practiced
chop, even that's gone now.

Two days of rain across time
and space, a hundred miles
of swirled cloud over flat water
moving north, northwest. That's
us, North. The land on this slow
spinning meteorology, a pinprick
on the Doppler of the weather channel.

## Santa Claus Saves Child in Pensacola Mall

It's a gift.
So often, everything is out of my hands.
The flying reindeer—it just happened.
I didn't breed or train them.
Didn't cast a spell. One day
the lead deer lifted off the crusted snow
like a paper airplane in the wind.
The others followed. We were flying
in the stars.

And the kids, I try
to make them behave, but coal
or cinders, it's not my call. Free
will, I guess. That old curse.
So many times the gap between
what a child wants and gets
is too vast for any saint or santa
to fill. I do my best, but resources
are limited and distribution seems,
at best, inefficient. After hundreds
of years of trying, so few have so much,
so many, so little. I've asked
for help, but it all seems ordained
by someone I can't see.

But that child—right there
in my hands—I made him breathe.
There was nothing to get in my way—
no fate, chance, free markets, welfare,
profit margins, downsizing...

And then, in just minutes—
Manila, the charred bodies of orphans, smoke
rising like a desperate offering, ashes
falling in a warm Christmas rain.

# The Grave

I throw in some old socks, something
that has traveled roads with me

I throw in a picture of me
as I am now, since soon I will change

I throw in a picture of me at age six
so I will always be there

I let them worry each other

I throw in a song without music
so it will be silent

I throw in words without a song
so it will have desire

I throw in a blue coffee cup
so the young boy and the words
will someday swirl together

## Letters Home: Travel. Spring. West. Elevation

For a week now I have awakened each morning in a different
state (except those two mornings in Texas–it's so
                                        fucking big)

to white walls and drawn curtains. Cheap rooms don't have clocks
and the light is different each day. I turn on the TV and look for
the weather channel. Digital time flashes below the map, and its childish

weather symbols. Little snowflakes in the Northeast. A green blotch
on Colorado. Sunbeam in the Arizona desert. Home, Florida
has its own permanent sun. It takes a moment to

remember where I am and what weather I'm looking for.  Forecasts
hardly work for me since it's elevation that brings the cold. The weather
channel man, safe in his Eastern perch knows the temperature

in Albuquerque, but not that it's snowing in Santa Fe,
Cortez, and Durango. He doesn't tell me
how cold it was atop Mesa Verde or whether ice pockets

dot the Canyonlands. Did he know that it was 18 degrees
at the Grand Canyon's rim? Last night a train ran
through my dreams and I woke next to the Flagstaff rail

yard. In Santa Fe the wind howled all night and snow piled on my car.
I wake in the same white room with light sliding beneath the thick
rubberbacked curtains. Sometimes the dawn, sometimes the security lights.

## The War, on Many Fronts

Why write a new poem for this war?
Throw good words after blood?

Why not quote Eberhart's fury,
Jarrell's washed out gunner?

Halfway through radiation, my neck
Reddens, peels, dries to ash.

My breath's scorched. Stomach
Queasy. I'm fighting

But with love. Chanting
Under my mask. Trying

To see the Medicine Buddha
With my eyes closed.

Counting the weeks and wondering
If our attack will begin

When I am flat on the table.
My president knows nothing

Of words, maybe of love
Either. On the drive home

From the hospital, I stop
To retch by a tulip magnolia

Pink with blossoms, the first
Of this early season. Our garden's

Still in winter vegetables: cabbage,
Kale, carrots, greens. No sign

Yet of spring. The woods are gray,
And I can see across the creek

Della and Callie running—
Blonde hair, blue shirts—

In Max's rye grass—emerald
Oasis where war will not rain.

There's still some hope
In the woodpecker's knock,

The finch at the feeder; even
Buzzards wheeling the sky

Are not metaphors for bombers
Shrieking for Bagdad. These are words

Of healing
But the sick cannot see

And their hearts, merely pumps,
Derricks in the sand.

## A Sign for Rain

Azaleas seem the first to wilt. The road's
yellow dust floats through the trees. Dogwood
leaves turn their backs on us.
Three years of drought changes the land.
The umbrella of every summer day's lost
on the floor of the car. Even the mildew
that marked our endless rot and wither

is a complaint I would welcome home.
Our forests are burning again.
Last summer smoke from Goose Bay
hung in the southern sky, but the lake between us
was our savior. The summer before my cousin's house
burned as the fires roared across the scrub plain.

When I was young I would have thought this perfect
beach weather. No lightning driving us from the water, no
rain puddling the seats of my car with its careless windows
down. Today, I ask the elders for help. Make it fall. Let fat drops
splatter this page, stain these words that fork no lasting sustenance.
Forgive my awkward theft. Come down here with the rain. Turn

your face to the sky. Let the first drops caress your forehead, drip
down your nose. Let's run naked through the pine straw,
leap through the lettuce, and roll in the mint. Wet dogs
at our heels, we'll listen to rain crash the magnolias. We'll dance
to the creek, water from the culvert, gullies and steepheads
swelling brown and muddy, as the creek overflows its banks.

# Elegy for Matthew Shepard

Strung, bleeding, broken—on a wind fence you die.
Don't ask. Don't tell what harm you could do.
Gay boy. The cold prairie never asks you why.

The wind here wears men down to dust and lies.
Finds you a scarecrow tied to a post, night ice blue.
Strung, bleeding, broken—on a wind fence you die.

That night after the drinks were you too high
To see it's a man's job to suffer, fight and screw
Up a gay boy? The cold prairie never asks why.

Out here, so odd, so queer who could deny
The long cold nights are longer for men like you.
Strung, bleeding, broken—on a wind fence you die.

There was never enough love for these drunken guys
Daddy gone. They fuck their girlfriends, then you.
A gay boy. The cold prairie never asks why.

Did you touch him? Look him too long in the eye?
Push him to the edge of what he long wanted to do?
Strung, bleeding, broken—on a wind fence you die.
Gay Boy. The cold prairie still asks us why.

# Alligator

There is no alligator
when the first dog
chases a bird in the water.

No alligator
when you wade in,
silt and mud warm as July.

No alligator you can see
as you hold your daughter's
hand.

There's no alligator for the first
twenty minutes, though a cooter
almost has you gathering

everyone to shore. There's
always an alligator you can feel.
You don't need the

warning sign
to make you believe. Then
outside the buoy rope,

the arbitrary boundary
of your world and theirs,
the alligator drifts.

You look hard. You want it
to be a log, but you know
it's the alligator you've been

waiting for. You know
you should not have come here,
dogs and daughter in tow;

you know luck is just a reprieve.
You send your daughter to the shore,
hold the lab by her thick roll of yellow fur.

The alligator rides outside the rope,
closes the gap only a few feet. Dogs
leashed, you climb the hill to the car.

You drive home listening to the valves
tick too loudly, to the air leaking
out of your tires, to the brakes

wearing  toward failure. The world's
alligator is there, slit eyes
just above the green water.

## Clearing the Air

My father died with all he believed in
still too much intact, and I live on now,
not worrying about how to bring him to me
or me to loving him. I had a father
and I didn't want him. When
he was gone I landed
one more time in Pittsburgh's
gray morning and rolled over the hill
to the river. I walked into the same
funeral home my grandfather,
grandmother, two step-brothers,
other souls less known to me
had slept beneath the pallid lights
and strewn flowers.

None of the stories of how they loved him
were mine. I had no story.
I looked at the gray old man
whose heart had exploded.
The honor guard marched in,
all but one old enough to be dead
for years, and said their military farewell.
I was on foreign soil, as always,
in his life and mine.
But he was leaving and the world
was now before me.
I do not gloat or celebrate,
there's enough lost to last
two lifetimes.

# Ghost Crabs

*for Wendy (and Dean)*

I have to confess this to you.
When you died it was the first time
I was really scared. I told
everyone I was getting better;
even you when I saw you,
frail, wrapped in a blanket, hair shorn short.
Then the call came that you were dead,
and this is selfish, but I knew I could die
too. I've been no good to anyone
who loved you. Here, tonight,
Dean was with you.

Here alone, I know
you're gone. I don't know what
I believe about where you are,
where we all might go.
As I walked the beach in the half-moon
light, ghost crabs covered the sand.
I played my light before me, afraid they'd run
over my bare feet. Some ran, some stopped and stared
up at me. Then I walked in the moon's faint glow,
trusted that the crabs would stay away from me,
that the moon can show us how to go home.

# Letters Home: Spring Storm, Santa Fe

*for M*

You would have hated this.
Cold wind blowing across the mountains,
juniper whipping at the edge of the rest area's
locked bathroom. Thick gray clouds.
The wind followed me down the valley
to the streets of Santa Fe,
blowing the wet promise of snow
around corners and down alleys.
I stepped over puddles, past
the closed store fronts of rich blue
and silver, silent museums of trinkets
and blankets. In the dark, adobe caught
the wind and pushed me toward the lights
of the plaza and the promise of warmth.
Out of season, most things closed,
I found a steamy restaurant of Mexican food,
and the waiter was so kind to me
that I knew I must have sat awkward, a man
with fogged glasses eating alone 2000 miles
from home. I walked along the Rio Grande,
snow clinging to steep stone banks
and thought how I need you here in summer
so I could belong to the galleries and expensive shops,
walk into restaurants and bars too rich
for my steel blood. You would have hated this:
the cold streets, me clenching my sooty dreams,
sure I did not belong. Snow blew
through the motel's security lights
and whipped across the kidney swimming pool.
I'm too early. Here in high country, it's elevation
and wind that makes the weather.
I'm only good when I'm driving. Tomorrow,
Mesa Verde, then Canyonlands. I'll stay in the sun.

## Shovel Handles in the Age of Terrorism

The dogs had a big possum
that looked dead, curled and silent. I took
it to the woods and began to dig, but this low buzzing
kept stopping me. I checked my pockets, the phone.
I looked at the sky then realized that the shovel handle
was vibrating from carpenter bees' long toil.
Do they drill to nest or to take
sawdust somewhere else? Miners
or builders? Either way they seem bent
on the destruction of our garden tools. They
hate our freedom to choose from square point,
round point, nursery spade.

They hate most the specialized things
we buy from late night TV—the multi
pronged golden tool that twists weeds
from the earth so we don't have to bend over
except when it does not work. They
hate the little plow with its bicycle tire.
They hate the bush ax, maddox, maul,
sledge hammer; the post hole diggers,
each splayed handle. They hate too
our houses. Our doors that let us in
and out. The evidence of their cells

is scattered on our sills and porches. They create
diversions in the city of vines and roots
and then the possum rises from its desperate
playing dead and staggers toward thicker
underbrush. I bang the shovel on a thick
sweet gum and the buzzing
subsides. I watch the possum safely away

to where its true fate waits. We do not hate
the possum; it's our nature to patrol our land,
to chase squirrels and deer, to bark
at the armadillo crashing through the night.

It's our nature to tree the peacocks
and the wandering guinea hens.
The copperhead strikes my dog's nose,
the moccasin bites her leg; the rabbit
lies down with the dog, but only
the dog rises again. The carpenter bee will drill
its holes tomorrow in our proffered tools,
our sacred house. In our sleep
all the world hums.

IV

## Bad Angels

Every two months the doctor slides
a camera, head small as a philosopher's
pin, into my nose and looks for the angels
dancing inside me. He's looking for the bad
angels, little Lucifers who have turned
away from their mission of good and now
run rampant—desire to rule overriding
                              their nature to serve.

I'm making this up. I never speak
like this to the doctor. What he knows
of angels, or imagination, I don't know.
I stiffen as the thin black snake
with its glistening eye
comes near me. I close my eyes
as it enters and wiggles through
my nose. I am not making
this up. Not all of it.

He says my throat looks less raw
than last time. No signs of cancer.
I'm happy to take him
at his word. I'm healing. I'm cautious
about saying this to the wind
or the morning light that listens.
To assume my health's guaranteed,
seems a necessary flaw. When the wind blows,
yesterday's rain drips from the trees in drops
almost singular. I'm not making this up.

# Anesthesia and Knives

### 1

I'm not lost but traveling.
Eyes closed under my mask
of mesh. I could be a scarecrow.
The goalie at death's net.

I imagine radiation
a pink-gray sun

descending. The tentacles
of a jellyfish wrapped around

my face, my throat, choking me.
Then it backs off, floats away.

If this is salvation, it's
slim and meager.

### 2

Body and soul
intertwined now, finally.

It took this. They are one
and sick. My soul

is my stomach, bile
rising in my throat.

My throat has closed;
it will not sing or swallow.

It feels only this dry pain.
I'm growing smaller.

I eat through a tube
that enters my stomach

like cable TV
without a picture.

This happens for far too long.
I'm not sure what I am.

Summer drags through daily rain.
Every day I say I'm a little better.

I might be. Measuring days,
swallows, broth. Looking

for what my throat
will admit.


3

"I'm slowly getting better,"
I write. My friend says

I am redefining slowly.
Not as fast as a snail. Not

as quick as a glacier's advance.
Not as slow as the progress

of justice. Not as certain
as the entry of the meek into heaven.

Nine months after surgery
I begin to begin again. Slowly,

I have come home. Every day
I rub my neck and check for lumps, but

I don't imagine each tick of scar tissue
a tumor. I measure my days

and find them glistening. I sing bass now;
all I've lost is my Frankie Valli and immortality....

*You're just too good to be true*
*Can't take my eyes off of you...*
*You'd be like heaven to touch*
*I wanna hold you so much*

# Heart

My heart was suspect.
Wired to an EKG,
I walked a treadmill
that measured my ebb
and flow, tracked isotopes
that ploughed my veins,
looked for a constancy
I've hardly ever found.
For a month I worried
as I climbed the stairs
to my office. The mortality
I never believed in
was here now. They
say my heart's ok,
just high cholesterol, but
I know my heart's a house
someone has broken into,
a room you come back
to and know some stranger
with bad intent has been there
and touched all that you love. You know
he can come back. It's his call,
his house now.

# Letters Home: Kuaa Pueblo

*to M*

You would have loved this:
these ruins where Coronado
wintered, the northern tether of Fray Marcos'
delusions. I walked the village
under sierra and sun. Francisco
found all of this—El Rio De Norte, Nuestra Senora,
the Rio Grande flowing fast and shallow,
snow hanging on the shoulders of the mountains—
but it wasn't enough.
I sat in a kiva where kachinas danced
on mud walls and thought of you—home
where dogwood and pear blossoms
were waking and the azaleas on fire.
It's brown here under the earth, and above too
the land is months from green.
I climbed the lodgepole
into the sun, as the young men must have
500 years ago when the blue sky greeted them
and the mountains rose up like home.
Down in Culiacán, Coronado's
army gathered like locusts,
then followed the rivers north.
This road runs west to Four Corners,
another north to Cortez. The next postcard
will tell which fork I choose.

## (a dream I had one night in America)

a long train of coal and chemicals, cattle, corn and steel strung
across the Midwest from Chicago to Wichita, carrying
the lives of those yet to come

and the ashes of those who died in the mines and mills, in fields
of wheat and cotton, in the cane when the rattlesnake flashes
from chopped stalks and sinks its fangs in the bare brown calf,

when the full weight of all God's great disparities falls
on the heads of Kentucky miners, their last light wavering
in the thick dust,

or those textile mills in the Carolinas,
the doors locked from the outside to keep
organizers out while flames sweep from loom to loom,

leap from dress to dress, char the bones
of women who scrape and claw barred doors.
We march through the streets

of Lowell and Paterson, through Haymarket,
Homestead, Bisbee and Bethlehem,
straight into the teeth of billy clubs,

the dogs of war; the steel hooves of horses
rear and smash us down. Broken now, all too human,
we cry in the future of shall and will and hope.

# Time Running Out on the Millennium

Time hardly matters anymore.
It's light that I reckon, light
or the lack of light that decides my days.
And trees, leaved or bare. The earth,
green or brown.

In Tibet,
or the Hebrew calendar,
the numbers, like spokes
on a roulette wheel, point
to another fortune.

The universe is four years old
like my daughter.
I was born in the year of Eisenhower.
In the foreshadowing of Nixon.
Bombs falling on Cambodia.
Students dead at Kent State.

Carter was President when I drove
a 66 Ford wagon home,
giving up Pennsylvania, West Virginia,
the twisting hills, gray rivers, mines
and mountains of my mother.

That car, rusted frame welded
by a biker near Erie,
Coke cans wired round the pipes,
boomed through Tennessee and Georgia
down the long sandy shoulder
of Florida, until the frame speared

the earth in the woods
behind my brother's warehouse;
we left it there, memorial,
to a job done well enough.

Now, I measure the past by how much
I remember. Measure distance
by my drive from town. Measure the sun
by its height in my windshield.
Measure joy by each time the gate
swings open and my daughter
runs up, flanked by dogs.

# Artifacts of Impermanence

Green spring
Brown fall

Wet paw prints
on a dusty floor.

Prayer flags fading
in the sun

Sophie shining
in the wet woods

The branch of the wild cherry
cracked, sprawled across the oak

The blighted pines
yellowed where the bark's fallen

Sometimes love and trust
The point of this pencil

The beat of my mother's heart
The swollen creek after rain

Ripe blueberries. The gauzy
light of the sun rising behind

The sweet gum
One magnolia blossom

# Trying to Save You

*for M, again*

Your closet is full of old sweaters,
the floor full of shoes and boots.

We still have Della's stroller
though she's now six

We have the papers from your old
life. Something's always lost
or about to be.

When the armadillo digs in your garden
it digs up your soul.

As our daughter grows to a young girl
you lose your baby

When the sun goes down
darkness rises

It's not a fair trade.

When I look into the night before sleep
I can't find your road home.

I can't keep the house from flying away.

# Burning Poems After the Contest's Over

It takes a lot longer to burn poetry
than to write it. One poem
goes up pretty quickly; edges
brown, then leap into flame.

Whole manuscripts resist
destruction, bundled pages
protect each other, insulate
lines of bad metaphors from flame.

O, it burns, but you have to push, prod,
tear and break it up, soon enough
it's gray, papery ash. Sometimes
a piece flutters off in the wind

like a moth. Maybe it's the odd
good simile freed from its more homely
companions. It's cold today.
Thanksgiving; while a duck bastes

in the oven, I worry about fire, stay close
to these poems that made little happen
when they were alive, but burning,
floating, they could catch pine straw afire.

The wind from the south could float
them to the house. So I poke
poems into flames. Even the least
poem has this alchemy, this

propensity to change. Long
into the night smoke will cling
to pine, seep through our sills,
wrap its faint lines through our sleep.

## Poetry Makes Nothing Happen

I want to claim that I don't understand genocide,
That I have not read history; that I don't
Understand the circulation of the blood
And how we can die from its
Spilling on the ground
From hacked off limbs.

I am against genocide
But who is for it? Do
Those who murder in genocide's
Name, favor it? Do they say
*I am a genocidist? I fly*
*The flag of genocide. I sever*
*Your wife's head in the name*
*Of genocide.*

Do they even say *I hate you?*
*I killed you because you're not like me.*
*You are too much like me.*

And how, if we go back
Can I not understand Wounded Knee,
The Trail of Tears, Manifest Destiny,
Major Mason's massacre of the Pequot?

How can I forget lynching,
Carpet bombing, Napalm, My Lai?
How can we go back?

*Poetry makes nothing happen,*
Auden so famously said. Yet
We are here, often. Ready to stop
The war, to end Apartheid, to bring
About justice.

We will rail and weep in verse
Against other atrocities, against air-
Tight containers of Chinese immigrants,
Trailers of dead Mexicans in the big armed
Cactus of the Sonora.

We will gather again.

# Prayer for Daily Neglects

*Supply for the good I ought to have done,*
*and that I have neglected this day and all of my life*

The broken pole
on Della's swing set

The redbud growing
too close to the pumphouse

The deck, mildewed,
dry rot

Pine straw carpeting the roof,
clogging the gutters

The dead loblolly leaning
toward the gazebo

The firepit
without a grill

The unpainted walls
of the tool shed

The tune up, the check engine
light, the unrotated tires

The broken window,
the unmopped floors

The fence that needs stringing
the azaleas that need pruned

The hoses that need coiled
the firewood that needs stacked

The dogs that need brushed
The birds that need names

My life, my life
The grass, the grass

## Design and Production

Text and cover design by Kathy Boykowycz

Text set in ITC Giovanni, designed in 1989 by Robert Slimbach
Titles set in Frutiger, designed in 1975 by Adrian Frutiger

Printed by Thomson-Shore of Dexter, Michigan,
on Nature's Natural, a 50% recycled paper